I0482609

Daylight and Midnight Symmetry Patterns

Quick Easy Fun Coloring For Grown Ups!

Copyright © 2016 Kelly Dombrowski

All rights reserved. No part of this book may be reproduced in any form by any electronic or mechanical means including photocopying, recording, or information storage and retrieval without permission in writing from the author.

ISBN-13: 978-1532976636

ISBN-10: 1532976631

www.ColoringBookNut.com

Printed in U.S.A

Daylight and Midnight Symmetry Patterns

Quick Easy Fun Coloring For Grown Ups!

by Kelly Dombrowski

How to Use This Book

If you choose to use markers or any medium that will bleed through to the other side, copy and print on card stock. You have permission to reproduce the pages for your personal use. You can try coloring them several different ways!

Most of all, have fun. If the spaces are too small, leave them white. If you need to do something, touch them up with a black fine tip marker. Don't fuss over how to fill those spaces! Color the fine lines on the ones with black backgrounds with marker or sparkly gel pens for some quick fun! Use neon colors for a color punch!

Relax and have your favorite drink or snack nearby. Put on some music or listen to your favorite TV show and color! Enjoy the process!

Never mind those lines. If you go over them, no one cares, you are enjoying yourself! And sometimes it's good therapy just to color with any old color that you fancy at the time! You don't need to show any of your work to anyone.

If you wish to improve, over time you will get better! Everyone can learn how to color like a professional with practice.

My hope is that this will be a gateway to more creative endeavors! Maybe someday you will try drawing your coloring pages or pick up a paint brush and start painting!

Visit *www.ColoringBookNut.com* for color ideas tips and tricks!

Have Fun!!

Visit us on social media! Show us what you have done and
let us share your awesome coloring skills!

 www.ColoringBookNut.com

 The Coloring Book Nut

 @KellytheArtist

 Kelly Dombrowski

 KellyDombrowskiArt

 The Coloring Book Nut

Look for these and other books by Kelly Dombrowski on Amazon.com

Kaleidoscopes Unleashed: An Adventure in Adult Coloring
Beginner Volume 1

Kaleidoscopes Unleashed: An Adventure in Adult Coloring
Intermediate Volume 1

Kaleidoscopes Unleashed: An Adventure in Adult Coloring
Advanced Volume 1

Sweet Curly Cue Designs: An Adventure in Adult Coloring
Volume 1

Sweet Curly Cue Designs: An Adventure in Adult Coloring
Volume 2

Powerful Positive Affirmations Adult Coloring Book:
Coloring for Health, Happiness and Wholeness

Inspirational Positive Affirmations Adult Coloring Book:
Nurturing and Loving Words to Feed Your Soul

Marvelous Symmetry Patterns Coloring Book for Grown Ups

Sweet Curly Cue Designs Volume 1
By Kelly Dombrowski

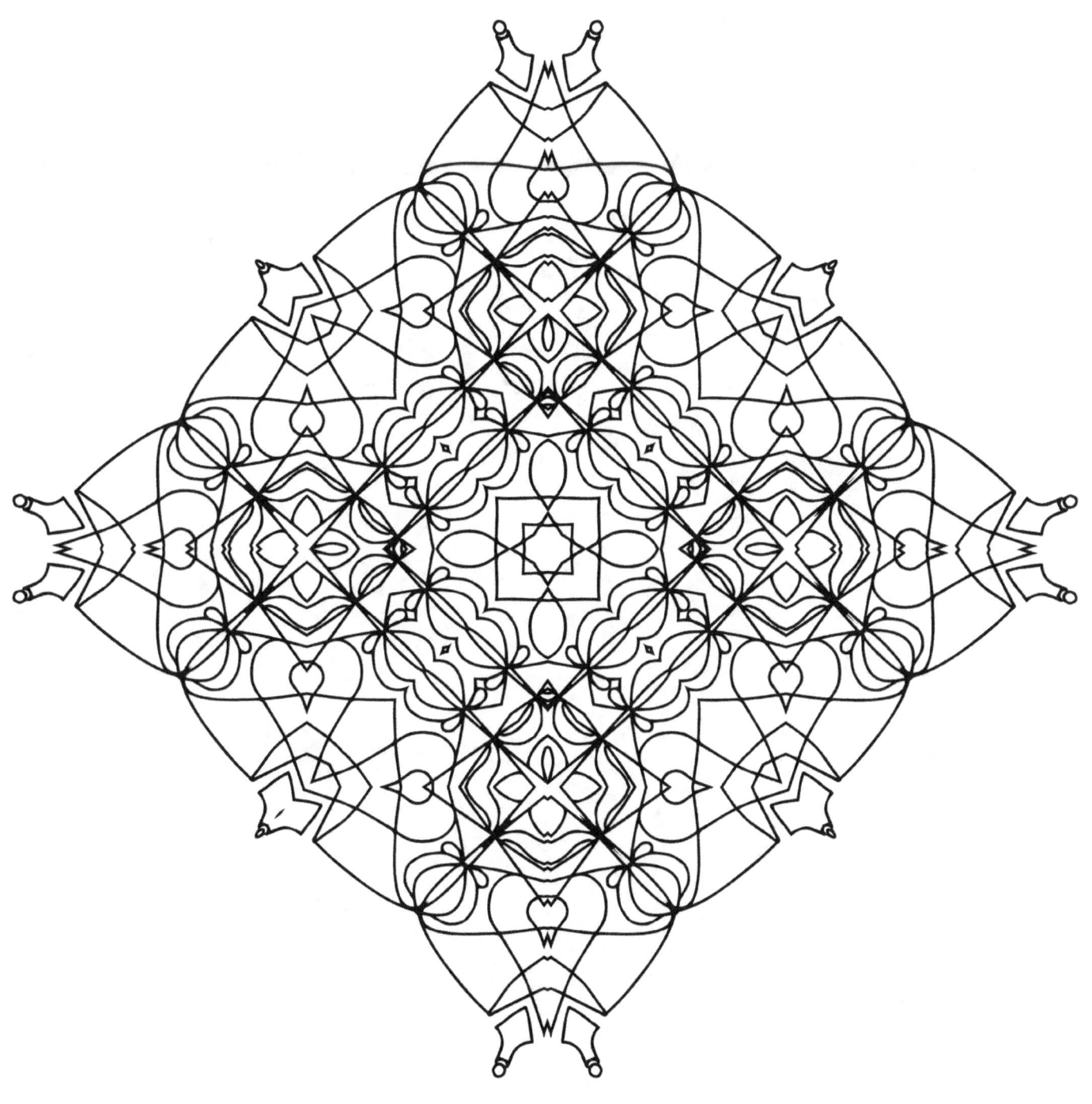

Kaleidoscopes Unleashed Advanced Volume 1
by Kelly Dombrowski

I Am

Fearless

Powerful Positive Affirmations by Kelly Dombrowski

www.ingramcontent.com/pod-product-compliance
Lightning Source LLC
Chambersburg PA
CBHW081608200526
45169CB00021B/2387